Volcanoes of the World™

Mount Vesuvius
Europe's Mighty Volcano of Smoke and Ash

Kathy Furgang

The Rosen Publishing Group's
PowerKids Press™
New York

For Adam

Published in 2001 by The Rosen Publishing Group, Inc.
29 East 21st Street, New York, NY 10010

First Edition

Series and Book Design: Michael Caroleo

Photo Credits: Cover image © North Carolina Museum of Art/CORBIS; title page, p. 16 © Archivo Inconografico, S.A./Corbis; p. 4 © Ente Nazionale Italiano Per Il Turismo; pp. 6, 15, 21 © Corbis; pp. 9, 10, 18, 19 © National Geographic; pp. 7, 8 by Michael J. Caroleo; p. 11 © Woods Hole Oceanographic Institution; p. 12 (Italian farmer) © Roger Ressmeyer/CORBIS; p. 12 (background) © Charles O'Rear/CORBIS; p.20 © Betmann/CORBIS.

Furgang, Kathy.
    Mount Vesuvius : Europe's mighty volcano of smoke and ash / Kathy Furgang.
      p. cm.—- (Volcanoes of the world)
    Includes index.
    Summary: This book describes the formation of Mount Vesuvius, one of the most famous volcanoes in the world, and tells of the 79 A. D. eruption which destroyed the city of Pompeii.
    ISBN 0-8239-5658-X
    1. Vesuvius (Italy)—Eruption, 79—Juvenile literature. 2. Volcanoes—Italy—Juvenile literature. [1. Vesuvius (Italy)—Eruption, 79. 2. Volcanoes.] I. Title.
II. Series.
2000
551.21—dc21

Manufactured in the United States of America

Contents

Naples and its volcano Mount Vesuvius are visited by people from around the world.

Mighty Mount Vesuvius

People from around the world like to visit Naples, a city in southern Italy. Naples is known for its ancient castles and its great food. Spaghetti and pizza were both invented in Naples! Not far from this busy city, however, is a powerful and dangerous volcano. Mount Vesuvius is one of the most famous volcanoes in the world. The mountain stands over 4,000 feet (1,219 m) tall. The distance around the base, or bottom, of the mountain is 30 miles (48.3 km). In the past, the volcano has blasted smoke, mud, and rock high into the air. Mount Vesuvius reminds the people living in Naples of the harmful power of nature.

What Is a Volcano?

To understand what a volcano is, you must first know what is inside our planet Earth. Earth has three layers. We live on the outside layer, called the **crust**. This layer is made of solid rock. The **mantle** is a layer of Earth that extends miles below the crust. The mantle is made of solid and liquid rock. The very center of Earth is called the **core.** Most of the core is made of solid and liquid iron. The very center of the core is solid. Earth's core is so hot it heats the entire mantle. Temperatures in the core reach 10,300 degrees Fahrenheit (5,704 degrees C)! Sometimes the pressure from this hot rock makes a break in Earth's crust. This break allows hot **magma** to shoot up to Earth's surface. Magma is rock from the mantle that heats up and becomes liquid.

6

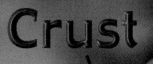

Crust

Mantle

Core

Magma

Earth's crust is 5 to 25 miles (8 to 40 km) thick. Its mantle is about 1,800 miles (2,900 km) thick. Earth's core is 2,150 miles (3,460 km) across.

Ocean

Continental Plate

Oceanic Plate

Magma

When two large plates push together or pull apart, they create a crack in Earth's crust. Layers of hot magma pour out of this crack and create a volcano.

Breaking Through Earth!

How does red, hot magma from deep inside Earth reach the surface where people live? Earth's crust is made up of large **plates**. These plates move very slowly. They move about two inches (5 cm) each year. That is less than the length of a large paper clip! A volcano is formed when two plates push together or pull apart to make a crack in Earth's crust. When hot magma from the mantle shoots up through this crack, an **eruption** occurs. Magma that reaches the surface of Earth is called **lava**. When lava cools, it becomes solid. Mount Vesuvius is made of layers of lava that have become solid.

When Mount Vesuvius Was a Baby

Earth is always moving and changing. It took about 300,000 years for Mount Vesuvius to look the way it does today. This volcano started out at the bottom of the ocean floor! Many of Earth's volcanoes are beneath ocean waters. These volcanoes are called **submarine volcanoes**. Each time Mount Vesuvius has erupted under the ocean, another layer of lava has been added to it. Volcanoes that form this way are called **stratovolcanoes**. Mount Vesuvius kept getting bigger and taller until it reached out of the ocean and became part of the coast of Italy. Lava from each eruption has made the volcano grow even higher. After hundreds of thousands of years, Mount Vesuvius finally became a mountain!

10

In this photograph, scientific tools measure a young stratovolcano that is being formed in the ocean.

Lava from Mount Vesuvius's eruptions made Earth's soil healthy for growing trees and plants like these grapevines.

The Somma Rim

About 17,000 years ago, Mount Vesuvius had already formed and had become a mountain. An eruption beneath Earth's surface caused Mount Vesuvius to collapse and cave in. The cave-in formed a crater, or hole, in the volcano. When a volcano forms a crater, it is called a **caldera**. Mount Vesuvius's caldera is called the Somma Rim. The mountain continues to grow out of that caldera. With each new eruption, lava pours out of Earth's surface. Although lava can be dangerous, it is rich in minerals. Today the caldera around Mount Vesuvius is covered with trees and plants. Farmers grow grapes in this area to make wine. Although we think of lava as dangerous, it is very healthy for Earth's soil.

Danger, Eruption!

When Mount Vesuvius erupted in the past, giant clouds of heavy smoke filled the air. The explosion blasted hot rock off the mountain forming tiny pieces called ash. Then the hot ash and smoke shot up high into the sky. The ash was carried away by the wind and settled on areas that were as far as 18 miles (29 km) away from the blast.

In the year 79 A.D., Mount Vesuvius had its most powerful eruption ever. The eruption buried three nearby towns. One of the towns, called Pompeii, was buried under 18 feet (5.5 m) of **rubble** and ash! Some of the most dangerous eruptions in the world have come from Mount Vesuvius.

This painting shows lava flowing and smoke and ash rising during an eruption of Mount Vesuvius.

This painting shows how an artist imagined the destruction of Pompeii during the eruption of Mount Vesuvius in 79 A.D.

The Big Blast

Mount Vesuvius was quiet for a very long time before the blast of 79 A.D. Imagine living in the year 79 A.D. and seeing Mount Vesuvius erupt. Many people did not even know what a volcano was! The eruption killed more than 2,000 people. A man named Pliny the Younger wrote letters about the event. He wrote that it was like a "storm of stones." Pliny the Younger was the first person ever to record information about volcanoes. Scientists now call this kind of smoky volcanic eruption **plinian**. Plinian eruptions were named after Pliny the Younger's uncle, a scientist who died in the blast. A plinian eruption is often the most violent kind. It is believed that the 79 A.D. eruption lasted for 19 hours and made a cloud of ash 20 miles (32.2 km) high.

Pompeii

The city of Pompeii seemed to completely disappear after being buried in the 79 A. D. Mount Vesuvius eruption. The buried city was discovered in 1748 by workmen who were digging a canal. Since then scientists have learned a lot about the way people died in the blast. It has taken more than 200 years to carefully uncover the city of Pompeii. Ash and mud had dried around the bodies of humans and animals. The ash had hardened into rock. Bodies were found in the same positions that the people had been in when they died. Mothers were holding their babies. People were in groups, huddled together. Scientists also learned a lot about how people in Pompeii had lived. They found homes, and many **artifacts**, or objects, that had been used by the people of ancient Italy.

18

Scientists used plaster to fill in the outline of a person who was caught in the 79 A.D. blast of Mount Vesuvius.

A jeep speeds away from the hot ash and smoke during the 1944 blast of Mount Vesuvius.

Many Eruptions

Mount Vesuvius has erupted many times. After the eruption of 79 A.D., the volcano erupted again in 1066, 1631, 1794, and 1906. The last time Mount Vesuvius erupted was in 1944. Each eruption killed many people and caused damage to the land around the mountain. Many smaller eruptions have also occurred. Is it time for another blast? Scientists do not know for sure. They have instruments that measure the movement of Earth's plates. Sometimes **earthquakes** are a warning that a volcano may erupt. Like volcanoes, earthquakes occur where the plates of Earth shift. When the plates below Mount Vesuvius move, it may cause another eruption.

Dangers Today?

Today Mount Vesuvius is a popular spot to visit. Houses have been built more than halfway up the mountain. The city of Naples is only a short distance away. Visitors travel to the mountain every day. What would happen if the volcano erupted today? Would people have enough time to be able to leave the area in time and find safety?

It is hard to tell what dangers lie ahead. People live in the area around Mount Vesuvius because they enjoy the mountain's great beauty. They know they cannot stop the powers of nature, so they enjoy its mystery and wonders instead.

Glossary

artifacts (AR-tih-fakts) Objects created or produced by humans.

caldera (kal-DEHR-ah) A crater formed by a volcano.

core (KOR) The hot center layer of Earth that is made of solid and liquid iron.

crust (KRUST) Earth's top layer of solid rock on which we live.

earthquakes (URTH-kwayks) Shaking or trembling of Earth's crust that happens when the movement of large pieces of land called plates run into each other.

eruption (ih-RUP-shun) The explosion of gases, smoke, ash, and lava from a volcano.

lava (LAH-vuh) Magma that flows out of a volcano during an eruption.

magma (MAG-muh) Hot liquid rock found in the mantle of Earth.

mantle (MAN-tuhl) The middle layer of Earth, between the crust and the core, that is made of solid rock and magma.

plates (PLAYTS) Large sections of Earth's crust that slowly move and shift.

plinian (PLIH-nee-in) A type of volcanic eruption that sends out large amounts of smoke and ash into the air.

rubble (RUH-bul) Broken parts of a building or other structure after it has collapsed.

stratovolcanoes (strah-toh-vol-KAY-nohz) Volcanoes that are formed by many layers of lava.

submarine volcanoes (sub-mahr-EEN vol-KAY-noz) Volcanoes that begin on the ocean floor.

Index

Web Sites

To learn more about volcanoes and Mount Vesuvius, check out these Web sites:

http://www.dgv.unina.it/vesuvio/quadreriahome.html
http://volcano.und.nodak.edu/vwdocs/kids/kids.html
http://users.netlink.com.au/~jhallett/volcanoes.htm